GRACE

Scripture Notebook

First published in Great Britain in 2023

Cover illustration by Hannah Green

Designed by Diane Warnes

ISBN: 978-1-915705-76-1

10Publishing a division of 10ofThose.com

Unit C, Tomlinson Road, Leyland, PR25 2DY, England

Email: info@10ofthose.com

Website: www.10ofthose.com

The Lord passed before him and proclaimed,
"The Lord, the Lord, a God merciful and gracious, slow to anger,
and abounding in steadfast love and faithfulness."

EXODUS 34:6

The L*ORD* *bless you and keep you;*
the L*ORD* *make his face to shine upon you and be gracious to you;*
the L*ORD* *lift up his countenance upon you and give you peace.*

NUMBERS 6:24–26

It was not because you were more in number than any other people that the LORD set his love on you and chose you, for you were the fewest of all peoples, but it is because the LORD loves you…

DEUTERONOMY 7:7–8

But the LORD was gracious to them and had compassion on them, and he turned toward them, because of his covenant with Abraham, Isaac, and Jacob…

2 KINGS 13:23

Nevertheless, in your great mercies you did not make an end of them or forsake them, for you are a gracious and merciful God.

NEHEMIAH 9:31

But as for me, I shall walk in my integrity;
redeem me, and be gracious to me.

PSALM 26:11

As for me, I said, "O Lord, be gracious to me;
heal me, for I have sinned against you!"

PSALM 41:4

For you, O Lord, are good and forgiving,
abounding in steadfast love to all who call upon you.
Give ear, O LORD, to my prayer; listen to my plea for grace.

PSALM 86:5–6

Light dawns in the darkness for the upright;
he is gracious, merciful, and righteous.

PSALM 112:4

O Lord, be gracious to us; we wait for you.
Be our arm every morning, our salvation in the time of trouble.

ISAIAH 33:2

Thus says the LORD*: "The people who survived the sword found grace in the wilderness; when Israel sought for rest, the* LORD *appeared to him from far away. I have loved you with an everlasting love; therefore I have continued my faithfulness to you."*

JEREMIAH 31:2–3

The steadfast love of the LORD *never ceases;*
his mercies never come to an end.

LAMENTATIONS 3:22

Who is a God like you, pardoning iniquity and passing over transgression for the remnant of his inheritance? He does not retain his anger forever, because he delights in steadfast love.

MICAH 7:18

And the Word became flesh and dwelt among us, and we have seen his glory, glory as of the only Son from the Father, full of grace and truth.

JOHN 1:14

For from his fullness we have all received, grace upon grace. For the law was given through Moses; grace and truth came through Jesus Christ.

JOHN 1:16–17

For all have sinned and fall short of the glory of God,
and are justified by his grace as a gift,
through the redemption that is in Christ Jesus.

ROMANS 3:23–24

For sin will have no dominion over you,
since you are not under law but under grace.

ROMANS 6:14

But by the grace of God I am what I am, and his grace toward me was not in vain. On the contrary, I worked harder than any of them, though it was not I, but the grace of God that is with me.

1 CORINTHIANS 15:10

For you know the grace of our Lord Jesus Christ,
that though he was rich, yet for your sake he became poor,
so that you by his poverty might become rich.

2 CORINTHIANS 8:9

The grace of the Lord Jesus Christ and the love of God and the fellowship of the Holy Spirit be with you all.

2 CORINTHIANS 13:14

Grace be with all who love our
Lord Jesus Christ with love incorruptible.

EPHESIANS 6:24

And the grace of our Lord overflowed for me with the faith and love that are in Christ Jesus. The saying is trustworthy and deserving of full acceptance, that Christ Jesus came into the world to save sinners, of whom I am the foremost.

1 TIMOTHY 1:14–15

Therefore do not be ashamed of the testimony about our Lord…
but share in suffering for the gospel by the power of God,
who saved us and called us to a holy calling, not because of
our works but because of his own purpose and grace…

2 TIMOTHY 1:8–9

He saved us, not because of works done by us in righteousness,
but according to his own mercy…

TITUS 3:5

But we see him who for a little while was made lower than the angels, namely Jesus, crowned with glory and honor because of the suffering of death, so that by the grace of God he might taste death for everyone.

HEBREWS 2:9

Let us then with confidence draw near to the throne of grace,
that we may receive mercy and find grace to help in time of need.

HEBREWS 4:16

But he gives more grace. Therefore it says,
"God opposes the proud but gives grace to the humble."

JAMES 4:6

Therefore, preparing your minds for action, and being sober-minded, set your hope fully on the grace that will be brought to you at the revelation of Jesus Christ.

1 PETER 1:13

And after you have suffered a little while, the God of all grace,
who has called you to his eternal glory in Christ,
will himself restore, confirm, strengthen, and establish you.

1 PETER 5:10

The grace of the Lord Jesus be with all.
Amen.

REVELATION 22:21